CRAFT AND ART

Sapperton and Oakridge
1902-1918

Acre Press

First edition May 2019

B

FOREWORD

For a few years at the beginning of the last
century the upper Chalford valley boasted
some very remarkable residents and visitors.
This booklet introduces those people and
looks at the sequence of events which led to
their coming. Much of the story is told in the
words of those artists, craftsmen and writers
themselves.

CONTENTS

William Morris

THE ARTS AND CRAFTS MOVEMENT

The damaging effect mechanization and mass production were having on design and decoration was recognized by social thinkers from the earliest days of the industrial revolution. Craftsmen whose creative use of wood, clay, metal and stone gave them pleasure and pride as well as an income were being replaced by poorly paid, regimented workers churning out standardized products with no say in the whole process and no scope for imagination or fulfilment, and inevitably the things produced in this way lacked grace and beauty. Poets like Oliver Goldsmith had been quick to point out the dehumanizing and ugly side of industrialization. But it took a long time for the concerns articulated by a few visionaries to gain traction and inspire any kind of counter-revolution. Meanwhile industrial design was left to factory owners and engineers, who had little interest in the social, moral and aesthetic aspects of production.

In the end the task of confronting the brutality of industrialization fell to architects, whose profession was the only one where the noble visions of an artist could be blended with the knowledge of an engineer and the practicality of a workman. The Gothic Revival pioneer Augustus Pugin was one of the first architects to lecture on the virtues of old traditional craftsmanship. Besides designing buildings and furniture he ran a workshop which produced handmade stained glass, metalwork, textiles and jewellery. John Ruskin provided a sound theoretical basis for the anti-industrialists, insisting that artefacts should reflect both the material they were made of and the person who created them, and that work should be fulfilment rather than drudgery. George Edmund Street, an architect based initially in Oxford, later in London, had similar ideas to Ruskin and exercised a strong influence on his followers who included William Morris, Philip Webb, John Dando Sedding and Norman Shaw. William Morris became the most vocal and influential representative of the anti-industrial trend, which under his leadership became widely known as the Arts and Crafts movement. Morris was a man of huge energy and ability: architect, poet, writer, lecturer, teacher, designer, craftsman, entrepreneur and publisher, and he was a passionate socialist.

"Life without industry is guilt, industry without art is brutality." – **John Ruskin**

"Have nothing in your houses that you do not know to be useful, or believe to be beautiful." – **William Morris**

Ernest Gimson's cottage in Sapperton
(etching by Frederick.Griggs)

THREE RADICAL YOUNG ARCHITECTS

Ernest Gimson, a young architecture student from Leicester, met the Arts and Crafts guru William Morris in 1884 when the latter visited the city to deliver a public lecture. Morris recognized Gimson's talent and kept in touch with him. When Gimson had completed his studies in Leicester Morris advised him to complete his professional formation at John Dando Sedding's practice in Oxford Street, London, which was next door to Morris' own business premises. There Gimson met the brothers Ernest and Sidney Barnsley who came from a prosperous Birmingham family; their grandfather had founded a successful construction firm and worked with Birmingham's celebrated neo-Gothic architect John Henry Chamberlain. Ernest Barnsley was Gimson's fellow apprentice at Sedding's studio, while Sidney was working under Norman Shaw. The three young architects took on board the ideas of John Ruskin, for example that the design and decoration of a building, or indeed of any artefact, should correspond to its location, the materials used in its construction and its purpose, and reflect the person or people involved in its creation. William Morris' theories regarding nature as a source of inspiration and creative manual work as essential to satisfaction and enrichment, were likewise passed on to them.

After they had completed their training both Ernest Gimson and Sidney Barnsley spent some time travelling and studying historic buildings. Then with William Lethaby[1] and others in London they formed a company, Kenton & Co, in which skilled cabinet makers were employed to produce good quality furniture. The venture was not unsuccessful, but was soon abandoned by mutual consent. By this time Gimson and Sidney Barnsley were convinced that in order to develop their ideas they needed to move to a rural area where local traditions of craftsmanship could be revived and nature would be at hand to provide inspiration and guidance. In 1893 they persuaded Ernest Barnsley to leave the practice he had started in the West Midlands and join them in setting up an Arts and Crafts operation some-where in the Cotswolds. They searched for a suitable site and eventually settled on Pinbury Park near Cirencester, a derelict property owned by Lord Bathurst, which they started renting in 1894. As well as producing furniture in the outhouses they restored the mansion and its grounds. In 1902 Lord and Lady Bathurst took over the property for their own use, but agreed to cover the full cost of rehousing each of the three artists in Sapperton, again on Bathurst land, in cottages they were invited to construct for themselves. They were also offered Daneway House, which Lord Bathurst had recently acquired, to use for workshops and showrooms, on the understanding that they would restore its fabric and interior.

Showroom inside Daneway House,
with samples of Ernest Gimson's furniture

THE SAPPERTON WORKSHOPS

Ernest Gimson and Ernest and Sidney Barnsley were gentlemen of means, and before their arrival in Gloucestershire they had had little experience of manual work. Now they became practical craftsmen. True to the principles underpinning the Arts and Crafts movement, the trio were as much concerned with the design and fabrication of furniture and fittings as with the construction of buildings. While at Pinbury all three of them had produced furniture with their own hands, Sidney Barnsley being at that stage the most assiduous in exploring techniques and establishing basic principles of design. Gimson also learned how to make ladderback chairs with rush seats and how to mould plaster by hand. Simplicity, truth to nature and harmony were the ideals they all aspired to in their work.

After moving to Sapperton each of the three began to forge his own way in accordance with his particular interests. Ernest Barnsley more or less ceased his connection with furniture production and applied himself almost entirely to building work. It was he who renovated Daneway House, and in the following years he took on numerous other architectural commissions of which the most important was the construction of Rodmarton Manor. Sidney Barnsley, on the other hand, remained committed to cabinet-making and took personal responsibility for the design and execution of every commission he accepted, working to a very high standard. On occasion he did also undertake some architectural work, an easily visible local example of which is the war memorial cross in Minchinhampton High Street.

Ernest Gimson, meanwhile, "with his far more active mind and wider interests", as Norman Jewson put it[2], concentrated most of his great energy on design, delegating the execution of his projects to the workers he employed and trained. Peter van der Waals, a cabinet-maker from Holland, was taken on as foreman to oversee the work of a team of furniture makers at Daneway House while under Gimson's careful guidance Alfred Bucknall, the son of a Tunley wheelwright, developed into a master metalworker and Edward Gardiner, son of the Daneway sawmill owner, became an expert maker of chairs. Gimson continued to do moulded plasterwork himself and, remarkably, he managed to find time for a certain amount of architectural work as well.

The Sapperton studios and workshops of Ernest Gimson and the Barnsley brothers were undoubtedly one of the most important centres of the Arts and Crafts movement in Britain before the Great War, and they quietly revolutionized furniture design.

Ernest Gimson

NORMAN JEWSON AND ERNEST GIMSON

In 1907 Norman Jewson, a young architect from Norwich, came to Sapperton to meet Ernest Gimson. He was hesitant and unsure of what kind of reception he would get, but Gimson was welcoming and sympathetic. The two men found that they shared the same outlook and interests, and Gimson happily took Jewson on as his assistant.[3] Jewson later drew a vivid picture of Gimson and his lifestyle:

> He was a tall, well-built man with a slight stoop, a large rather heavy face, except when he smiled, a brown moustache and wide-open contemplative eyes. His expression was that of a man entirely at peace with himself and all the world.[4]
>
> Gimson generally started the morning in his drawing-office. Then he dropped in for a short chat with Sidney at his workshop, after which he went on to the blacksmiths' shops. Most afternoons were spent in his drawing-office, but he walked across to Daneway two or three times a week. Work in the drawing-office was varied by afternoons in the open shed below when there was modelled plasterwork to be done. He was a tremendous walker and had once walked forty miles in a day with his long easy stride. He knew most bird calls, the homes of badgers and foxes, where the dipper nested and the red squirrel had his drey. A fine tree he admired as much as a fine building. Anecdotes of William Morris and Philip Webb, both of whom he had known in his London days, were interspersed with discussions on philosophy, folk-lore, the revival of the crafts, and almost every subject except politics and religion. His gospel was that of William Morris, of healthy employment for all in making useful and beautiful things or productive agriculture, giving everyone an intelligent interest in their work, time to do it as well as might be, with reasonable leisure time for other interests. He hated mechanisation in any form and would allow no machinery of any sort in his workshops, not even a circular saw. Tolerant of other people's ways of life, his own personal habits were carefully regulated, and not without a certain austerity. He preferred a rush-seated chair to an upholstered one, plain lime-washed walls to wallpapered, plain home-made food to imported luxuries. He loved all simple fun, good music and country dancing. He had a good baritone voice and enjoyed singing such songs as 'Turmut Hoeing,' 'The Leather Bottel' and a curious old local song called 'Tom Ridler's Oven' as well as many from Gilbert and Sullivan's operas.[5]

Alfred Powell's cottage at Gurners Farm
(photographed about a century later)

ALFRED POWELL

Alfred Powell was another of the young architects articled to John Dando Sedding's practice in London in the 1880s, and he had formed an enduring friendship with his fellow students Ernest Gimson and Ernest Barnsley, and Barnsley's younger brother Sidney. Like them he had broadened his interests to include design and craftwork alongside architecture as such. In 1901 he visited his three friends at Pinbury Park, and there tried his hand at chair-making with Ernest Gimson. However his *forte* was painting, and he had become an expert in ceramic decoration.

In 1902, at the time when Gimson and the Barnsleys were relocating from Pinbury to Sapperton, Powell bought a property in Oakridge Lynch called Gurners Farm. He restored its buildings and created an attractive cottage garden. This tribute written by a garden lover who visited the house in 1914 shows that Powell's creative skills were not limited to painting:

> Once, and once only, I have seen a garden which was in all senses and quite literally an artist's work. A well-known flower painter had for many years lived in that old Cotswold farmhouse, working his own orchard and garden as well as following his craft. As I look back on my first enchanted vision of the place [I recall] the perfect adjustment by which the artist, while keeping the necessary utilities of his plot, and the indestructible charm of that old house and its bearing fruit trees, wrought in just so much embroidery of flowers as made a harmony of the whole. [6]

Powell did not, in fact, live "many years" at Gurners Farm. Unlike the Sapperton craftsmen he kept up his links with London and spent much of his time in the capital. In 1904 he and his wife Louise set up a ceramic painting studio in London and they were then kept busy fulfilling orders from Wedgwood and training novices. They took to renting out part of Gurners Farm as a holiday home, and finally sold it in 1916.

Oakridge in those days was noticeably different from Sapperton in culture and atmosphere, as Norman Jewson observed:

> The valley even now is a sufficient obstacle to make communication between those living on the opposite sides of it comparatively rare, and to give a very different outlook to those of each side. At Sapperton our natural shopping centre is Cirencester, while Oakridge people all shop at Stroud as a matter of course. We tend to be conservative in outlook and politics; they used to be radical and now tend to be socialists. [7]

Sir William Rothenstein

WILLIAM ROTHENSTEIN

Among Alfred Powell's friends in London was William Rothenstein, a draughtsman and painter well known in artistic and literary circles, who was later to become the Principal of the Royal College of Art.[8] In his younger days he had spent time in Paris and associated with figures like Edgar Degas and Auguste Rodin. Though initially Rothenstein had limited interest in architecture and handicrafts he became increasingly attracted to the followers of William Morris, as he explained in his autobiography:

> I got into touch with the Arts and Crafts movement through Eric Gill, who taught stone carving at the Central School of Arts and Crafts, of which Lethaby[9] was Principal.
>
> Lethaby was an admirable Head; a sensitive architect and a great mediaeval scholar, who had, without seeming to exercise it, a powerful influence on his staff. These men were all practising craftsmen, and they gave to the school a part of their time only. Lethaby saw that crafts could be well taught only by men who are themselves masters of their craft.
>
> I was at once impressed by the atmosphere of good will and good workmanship at the Central School of Arts and Crafts; and there came to me a new interest and a new understanding for a side of art I had not yet appreciated. I learned much from Lethaby, Eric Gill, Edward Johnston, Halsey Ricardo and from Alfred Powell, too, whom I had met at Cambridge, and whose skilful painting on pottery I greatly admired.
>
> I began to see that the collecting of antiques was detrimental to living work; that the normal course was to have things made for one's own use by contemporary workmen. Nothing else would keep invention and good workmanship alive; and my instinctive dislike for 'the man of taste' seemed justified, now that I saw how much easier it is to pick out pleasant things from an antique shop, than to have sufficient knowledge and judgment to have things made expressly for one's needs.[10]

William Rothenstein, with his wife Alice and their four children, spent the summer of 1908 at a cottage in Througham, not far from Oakridge, and on that occasion Rothenstein made a point of going over to Sapperton to meet Ernest Gimson and the Barnsley brothers for the first time. Probably he had been urged to do so by Alfred Powell, who was the friend common to all of them. In 1912 Powell offered his cottage at Gurners Farm for rent, and the Rothensteins came down to spend another Gloucestershire summer in it.

At William Rothenstein's house in Hampstead:
Rabindranath Tagore (centre), William Rothenstein (standing, right);
between them is the young John Rothenstein,
and seated right is Rabindranath's son Rathindranath Tagore

THE CREATION OF *GITANJALI*

The English *Gitanjali*, which won Rabindranath Tagore the Nobel Prize for Literature, is dedicated to William Rothenstein. Rothenstein was largely responsible for getting the work written and bringing it to the attention of the English literary world, and Oakridge Lynch played a part in the story.

In his memoirs Rothenstein describes how, after reading one of Tagore's stories in translation, he wrote to the poet asking whether any more of his works were available in English. A member of Tagore's entourage responded by sending him translations of a few poems by Tagore, which much impressed Rothenstein. Rothenstein then invited Tagore to visit England, promising to introduce him to like-minded people.

> Then news came that Rabindranath was on his way. I eagerly awaited his visit. At last he arrived, accompanied by two friends, and by his son. As he entered the room he handed me a note-book in which, since I wished to know more of his poetry, he had made some translations during his passage from India. He begged that I would accept them.
>
> That evening I read the poems. Here was poetry of a new order which seemed to me on a level with that of the great mystics. Andrew Bradley[11], to whom I showed them, agreed: 'It looks as though we have at last found a great poet among us again,' he wrote.
>
> I sent word to Yeats[12], who failed to reply; but when I wrote again he asked me to send him the poems, and when he had read them his enthusiasm equalled mine. He came to London and went carefully through the poems, making here and there a suggestion, but leaving the original little changed. [13]

It was the summer of 1912. Rothenstein was renting Gurners Farm from Alfred Powell and he invited Tagore down to Oakridge. During his visit Tagore worked on some more translations while Rothenstein executed a series of pencil portraits of him. Those sketches are now in the National Portrait Gallery in London.

Rothenstein then asked Yeats to write an introduction for a collection of Tagore's translated poems. In due course Yeats wrote his introduction and the poems were published in a limited edition by the India Society, under the title *Gitanjali*. They were well received, and once the Macmillan company (at Rothenstein's insistence) had taken over publication the work was widely disseminated and Tagore's reputation in the Western world was assured.

Rabindranath Tagore
(pencil sketch by William Rothenstein)

TAGORE IN OAKRIDGE LYNCH

August 1912 was an exceptionally wet month and Rabindranath Tagore was unable to derive much pleasure from the local countryside. As a fastidious Bengali gentleman accustomed to dousing himself with several bucketfuls of fresh water every morning, he was disappointed by the almost non-existent bathing facilities at the farmhouse. The toilet arrangements he darkly refers to in this letter to his daughter were no doubt of a similarly crude nature.

Oakridge Lynch, Stroud, Gloucestershire

Miru,

Right now we are staying in a proper village in the house of a well-off farmer. His wife and daughter are looking after us well. The country is really beautiful here – only the weather is atrocious. The other major drawback is the lamentable arrangement for bathing and related activities. If instead something had been cut from my food rations, I would not have complained. But when in the morning there appears in my bedroom a bathtub resembling a rather large teacup and a container of water the size of a big teapot, I feel like making up for the lack of water with my tears. This must be quite the tiniest receptacle ever to call itself a bath. I shall omit to describe other essential facilities, because that would not be at all pleasant to hear.[14]

Tagore's friendship with Rothenstein subsisted, and according to Norman Jewson he visited the Rothenstein family again a few years later, after they had taken up residence in Far Oakridge:

Tagore came for a long visit to Iles Farm and while he was there we were invited with other friends to go over and hear him recite one of his longer poems. He was an impressive, if a shade theatrical, figure in his Eastern robes, as he read his poem in perfect English, by moonlight on the terrace in front of the house.[15]

Iles Green Farm after reconstruction
(painting by William Rothenstein)

A HOUSE IN FAR OAKRIDGE

William Rothenstein and his wife were so smitten by the beauty of the Golden Valley that they decided to make their home in Oakridge. In his memoirs Rothenstein explained how this came about.

> During the summer we spent in Gloucestershire my wife and I, walking one afternoon with Tagore, came upon an old farmhouse overlooking the Golden Valley. The house was in a state of decay; there was no gutter to gather the rain and the walls were soaked with damp. But we saw its great possibilities. My wife, impetuous as usual, said we must rescue the place. We made inquiries; the property belonged to a Miss Driver whose family owned most of the land thereabouts. She was willing to sell the house, with 55 acres, part of which was woodland, for £1300. I borrowed £1000 from my father, wrote out a cheque for £300 (my savings from my American journey) and became the possessor of a tiny estate. Oh the pride with which I first explored each field, and the lovely beech wood, and the house and barn! I was too ignorant to notice the lamentable state of the walls and fences.
>
> Built on the edge of the hill, the house, with its plain stone front and irregular mullioned windows, faced due south, opposite Sapperton and Frampton Mansell. An orchard fell away from it steeply, and below were fields and a fringe of beech wood running down to a canal, a proud engineering feat of the 18th century, and nearby was a tunnel which ran for four miles under Sapperton, hereabouts out of repair, through which barges could no longer pass. Nature had now taken possession, and everywhere weeds and rushes grew, and there were wild water-lilies, and kingfishers nested along the banks. Here and there a lock still held enough water, in which the children could bathe and fish. There were too many locks to be tended. Thus far and no further; man can say nay to nature, but he must not let go of that which he makes; so long as he watches over his handiwork nature respects it. At Chalford, two miles away, the canal was in use again, and boats were built between Chalford and Stroud. The old mills thereabouts with the millers' houses attached put me in mind of those near Bradford. There were many such at Chalford; and between Stroud and Painswick; and at [Longfords], where the Playnes lived, was an 18th-century mansion, with a mill in the park, telling of past prosperity. [16]

Norman Jewson
(pencil sketch by William Rothenstein)

RESTORING ILES GREEN FARM

Norman Jewson had joined Ernest Gimson as his assistant (for design work as well as for architectural drawing) in 1907. Jewson was an ardent admirer of Gimson's products, as he made clear in his memoir:

> Such furniture as Gimson's I had never seen before, which was no wonder, for although it was traditional to the extent of the use of the best craftsmanship in construction and finish, it was entirely original in design and had an assured distinction which only a master mind could have evolved. In its design, grace of form was combined with extreme simplicity to emphasise the beauty of the wood. Oak, mahogany, burr-elm and ebony were used in different pieces, each of which had its special treatment to bring out the full beauty of the material, while instead of hiding the construction, the perfectly made dove-tails wre allowed to make a natural pattern where they occurred. [17]

William Rothenstein engaged Norman Jewson as his architect to plan and oversee reconstruction work at Iles Green Farm in the traditional Cotswold style. In the course of this a misunderstanding arose between Rothenstein, the ebullient artist, and Ernest Gimson, the methodical master craftsman.

> Arthur Gardiner, the Sapperton carpenter, acted as builder, all the masons, stone tilers and carpenter being Oakridge men. Rothenstein suggested that one of Gimson's blacksmith's apprentices who lived at Oakridge should make the latches, hinges, casements and other ironwork required in his spare time, and at first I saw no harm in this, but when it was pointed out to me that the man had no workshop of his own and was making these things in Gimson's workshops, using his fuel and tools, of course I had to make a different arrangement. Unfortunately, I could never get Rothenstein to appreciate the necessity for the change. [18]

Rothenstein thought Gimson was simply being unhelpful, and for a while relations between the two of them were cool; but as neither of them was one to hold a grievance peace was ultimately restored. When the building work was done Rothenstein bought furniture from Sapperton.

> We got many pieces from Gimson, among others a cupboard, painted by Alfred Powell, with pictures of our house and the local landscape and flora and fauna, a delight to our children. I owe a debt to Gimson, and to the Barnsleys. [19]

André Gide
(sketch by William Rothenstein)

DISTINGUISHED VISITORS

William Rothenstein was a sociable person with numerous friends in the artistic circles of London and Paris. Among his more noteworthy visitors at Iles Farm were the artist Augustus John, the super-tramp poet W.H. Davies and the literary brothers A. E. Housman and Laurence Housman.

Two of the most illustrious figures to walk the lanes of Far Oakridge in Rothenstein's company were William Butler Yeats, the Irish poet, and André Gide, the French novelist. Unfortunately neither of them seems to have been deeply impressed by the local countryside.

> The poets in the country puzzled and amused me: I would take them to remote valleys, through flowering orchards and hanging beech woods, yet they never seemed to notice anything. Yeats would keep his eyes on the ground, and while Davies was with us he would talk literary gossip and ask my opinion of this or that poet, while cuckoos sang and rainbows arched the valley. [20]

Yeats inhabited the world of his imagination and at times could seem oblivious to his surroundings. Certainly no trace of the Cotswolds can be found in any of his poetry. Gide, too, who called on William Rothenstein while on a visit to England in 1918, had a head seething with social and moral questions and was more eager to talk than to go round admiring the beech woods.

> While he talked, I made a dozen drawings of him, some of which seemed to please him, for he pressed me to come to Paris, to make a set of French drawings; I must draw Proust, and others of his friends.
>
> Gide had a half satanic, half monk-like mien; he put one in mind of portraits of Baudelaire. Withal there was something exotic about him. He would appear in a red waistcoat, black velvet jacket and beige-coloured trousers and, in lieu of collar and tie, a loosely knotted scarf.
>
> I missed Gide when he left us. Such talk as his, so alert, so profound, gave me a nostalgia for Paris. [21]

Max Beerbohm

MAX BEERBOHM

One of the more eccentric and endearing of William Rothenstein's guests was the writer and caricaturist Max Beerbohm.

> From 1914 to 1918 Max Beerbohm lived in a cottage at Far Oakridge belonging to Sir Willam (then 'Will') Rothenstein, quite close to his home, Iles Farm. For part of that time I was altering Iles Farm for Rothenstein, and being very friendly with him and his charming family I was over there a great deal. Max spent much of his time at Iles Farm, as W.R. was one of his oldest friends, and he was devoted to the children, so it was my great good fortune to see him frequently while he was there. At first it amazed me to see him, in the depths of the country, in war time, always perfectly dressed as if for a garden party at Buckingham Palace, but as I got to know him better I realised that he just could not do anything else. [22]

> Lady Rothenstein had a story of him at the time he was staying at Oakridge. She and Mrs Beerbohm were out for a short walk, when a lark got up and started to sing. Mrs Beerbohm said at once that she must hurry back and fetch Max, because he had never heard a lark. But Max took so long finding his right gloves, cane, spats and hat for a country walk, that by the time they reached the field they sought, the lark was no longer to be seen or heard. [23]

It was while staying at Rothenstein's cottage that Max Beerbohm took a book out of the bookshelf one rainy afternoon, found it to be sloppily written and quite unreadable, and flung it onto the fire in a fit of disgust. He then spent an anxious hour trying unsuccessfully to make the flames complete the job of burning it, and feeling guilty at his own act of vandalism. This episode was the basis for an amusing short story he wrote entitled *The Crime*.[24]

Cottage Song, a doggerel poem written by John Drinkwater about Rothenstein's cottage ended thus:

> My path of paven grey / Is thoroughfare all day
> For fellowship, till time / Bids us with candles climb
> The little whitewashed stair / Above my lavender.

Max Beerbohm trumped it with his parody *Same Cottage, Another Song*:

> My path of cinders black / Had an abundant lack
> Of visitors, till time / Bade us with boxes climb
> The train that hurries on / To old warm Paddington. [25]

Mabel Dearmer

MABEL DEARMER

Mabel Dearmer, a restless creative soul, was by turns a book illustrator, author, dramatist, theatrical producer and costume hire agent. In the years before the Great War she was well known for her children's books and her play *The Cockyolly Bird*. Her life was cut short by the war, but immediately before that she enjoyed some of the happiest days of her life in Oakridge. A writer friend of hers recorded her first visit to the hamlet in rapturous terms:

Chance brought to her the fact that Mr. Alfred Powell, the painter of china, wanted to let his cottage in the Cotswolds, and she asked me to take a day off and go down with her to look at it. It must have been early in June that she climbed for the first time the steep footpath that leads up some three hundred feet from the Chale valley to the ridge on which is the church and village of Oakridge Lynch. We asked our way to Mr. Powell's house, and came to a door in a wall over which stood up the spiky leaves and burnished heads of tall artichokes; inside showed the roofs of, it seemed, half a dozen houses. We entered into a close of flowers, and as the door swung inwards it brushed against a great clump of thyme planted on purpose to send up welcoming odours. A few steps farther down the steep pathway pink roses were festooned across from one wall to a sheltering hedge of close-trimmed yew. Beyond that was the shaded porch, deeply sunk, and a mass of jasmine and clematis ran riot over it. The house itself was thatched with grey straw – not the traditional Cotswold roofing. But Cotswold stone made the solid block of its walls, and those mullioned windows which are Cotswold's special charm. The place looked south and east over a network of steeply cut valleys, rich in timber. All there was green and grey; but nearer the house was vivid colour – a mass of blue creeping veronica under the low windows and white pinks near them. It was an old farm remade by an artist craftsman: the garden was his creation, and the whole thing stood there a finished work – lovelier by far than any picture. Its two acres of steeply sloping ground were in orchard, but in front of the house, girded by a dry-stone wall, was a rolling space of roughly scythed lawn. All one could say was that the place was too pretty to be real. [26]

A cottage garden similar to the one at Gurners Farm

GOLDEN INTERLUDE

Having rented Alfred Powell's cottage Mabel Dearmer gleefully adopted the role of a crofter's wife.

> When the war broke out, I was at my cottage in the Cotswolds. It was a wonderful plum year, and every day each tree (not only in the orchard but on the lawn itself) tumbled its burden of purple fruit upon the ground. This meant work — work or wasps.
>
> At this time I hardly touched a newspaper. Every minute was occupied. From the early dawn, when, from my outdoor bed, I watched the sun rise through the tangle of flowers overtopped by gigantic hollyhocks to full mid-day, I was busy. I spent my whole day in the garden or orchard with Ann and William, the goats, and the two Skyes, Jacob and Oakridge Dorothy, and then on from full mid-day to the blue night, when the evening primroses lit their lamps and the night-jar just ruffled the air with his purring — on still into deeper night, when now and again a glow-worm sent a sudden signal, or the owls called sadly to one another across the transparent darkness — then sleep, and the glory of another day. [27]

Thiese lines written by Mabel's elder son Geoffrey Dearmer (who later made a name as a war poet) were inspired by Oakridge:

> The fields were loud with bees
> And drowsy with the wind-tossed meadow-sweet.
> From bowing trees
> Fell chatter, and above the garden wall
> Wide sunflowers beamed at spearing hollyhocks
> That dared the wind and scorned the clustered stocks
> And bore their laddered blooms high over all. [28]

The outbreak of the Great War in August 1914 abruptly ended an idyllic interlude. Though a pacifist Mabel Dearmer decided it was her duty to join the war effort. Her two sons enlisted in the army, her husband took leave from his parochial duties in London to become chaplain for a Red Cross unit in Serbia, and Mabel joined the same unit as a paramedic. She went out in April 1915, fell ill in June and died of typhoid fever and pneumonia in mid July. She was buried in Kragujevac.

Daneway House

AFTER THE WAR

Norman Jewson testified to the changes caused by the Great War.

> In the Cotswolds [before 1914] masons, carpenters and stone-tilers had all the traditional skill and pride in their work as their forefathers. The same could be said of the wheelwrights, blacksmiths, saddlers and other country craftsmen. Agricultural workers, too, were more highly skilled, while most of them had other crafts at their fingers' ends and could build a shed or a dry wall. Motor cars were still only rich men's toys and the only regular communication with the towns was by the weekly carrier's cart. In building, only horse-drawn transport being available, it was still the natural and cheapest way to use local materials. The stone came from the village quarry or was dug on the site; stone tiles for the roofs were quarried less than five miles away and oak and larch for the timbers could be had from the estate.
>
> After the 1914-18 war it was soon found that these simple ways had gone for ever. Many of the older and most highly skilled craftsmen had died or retired, while the younger men returned from the war had no sympathy with the old ways. Much of the traditional skill in building was gone, while with the coming of the motor lorry brickwork became cheaper than stone, and all kinds of manufactured materials were much more easily obtained. [29]

Gimson's death in August 1919 robbed the Sapperton crafts group of its greatest genius. The Daneway workshops closed down soon afterwards, though Peter van der Waals carried on their work, with many of the same employees, at an establishment he set up in Chalford. Ernest and Sidney Barnsley soldiered on, but they too were destined to die prematurely, just seven years after Gimson.

The legacy of Gimson and the Barnsley brothers remained, particularly in the area of furniture making. Their honest and imaginative approach to design influenced all subsequent workers in the field, and their innovative ideas were further developed in the Art Deco and Bauhaus movements. The Sapperton experiment, though short lived, had left its mark.

William Rothenstein moved back to London in 1920 when he became Principal of the Royal College of Art. However he and his wife returned to Far Oakridge after he had retired, as Sir William Rothenstein, in 1935.

Ernest Gimson, Ernest Barnsley and Sidney Barnsley are buried close together in Sapperton churchyard. William Rothenstein's grave is at the foot of the church tower in Oakridge Lynch, and there is an inscription to commemorate Mabel Dearmer at the village war memorial.

BIODATA

Pioneers of the Gothic Revival and Domestic Revival

Augustus Pugin, architect (1812-1852)
John Ruskin, artist and social philosopher (1819-1900)
John Henry Chamberlain, architect (1831-1883)
George Edmund Street, architect (1824-1881)
Philip Webb, architect (1831-1915)
Norman Shaw, architect (1831-1912)
John Dando Sedding, architect (1838-1891)

Members of the Arts and Crafts Movement

William Morris, architect, poet and craftsman (1834-1896)
William Lethaby, architect (1857-1931)
Ernest Gimson, architect and product designer (1864-1919)
Ernest Barnsley, architect (1863-1926)
Sidney Barnsley, architect and cabinet maker (1865-1926)
Alfred Powell, architect and ceramic painter (1865-1960)
Frederick Landseer Griggs, etcher (1876-1938)
Norman Jewson, architect and artist (1884-1975)

Others

Rabindranath Tagore, Bengali poet (1861-1941)
William Butler Yeats, Irish poet (1865-1939)
André Gide, French novelist (1869-1951)
William Rothenstein, draughtsman and painter (1872-1945)
Max Beerbohm, writer and caricaturist (1872-1956)
Mabel Dearmer, writer and dramatist (1872-1915)
Geoffrey Dearmer, poet (1893-1996)

NOTES

[1] William Lethaby, another architect, who had been Sidney Barnsley's fellow apprentice at Norman Shaw's practice in London.

[2] Norman Jewson, *By Chance I Did Rove*, 1973, page 22.

[3] Norman Jewson became one of Ernest Gimson's two faithful followers and friends, the other of whom was Frederick Griggs, a draughtsman and etcher. Jewson later married Ernest Barnsley's daughter Mary.

[4] Ibid, page 14.

[5] Ibid, pages 25-28 (extracts).

[6] Stephen Gwynn, *Garden Wisdom*, 1921, pages 108-109.

[7] Jewson 1973, page 52.

[8] He was also the father of Sir John Rothenstein, Director of the Tate Gallery from 1938 to 1964.

[9] William Lethaby the architect: see note 1.

[10] William Rothenstein, *Men and Memories*, 1932, Volume 2, pages 189-190.

[11] Andrew Cecil Bradley (1851-1935), literary critic and Shakespearean scholar.

[12] William Butler Yeats, the poet.

[13] Rothenstein 1932, Volume 2, Chapter XXX.

[14] Krishna Dutta and Andrew Robinson (editors), *Selected Letters of Rabindranath Tagore*, Cambridge University Press, 1997.

[15] Jewson 1973, pages 105-106.

[16] Rothenstein 1932, Volume 2, pages 272-273.

[17] Jewson 1973, page 12.

[18] Ibid, page 104.

[19] Rothenstein 1932, Volume 2, page 275.

[20] Ibid, page 341.

[21] Ibid, pages 343-344.

[22] Jewson 1973, page 106.

[23] Ibid, page 110.

[24] Ibid, pages 108-109;
Max Beerbohm, *And Even Now*, 1931, pages.245-253.

[25] Quoted in Rothenstein 1932, Volume 2, pages 324-325.

[26] Stephen Gwynn, *Memoir of the author* in *Letters from a Field Hospital*, 1916.

[27] Mabel Dearmer, *Letters from a Field Hospital*, 1916.

[28] Quoted in Stephen Gwynn, *Garden Wisdom*, 1921, page 48.

[29] Jewson 1973, pages 28-29.

Printed in Great Britain
by Amazon